Part Of The Series

Magical ME

Build A Healthy Relationship With Yourself

Dr Mariette Jansen

Published in 2023

ISBN: 9798859011858

Imprint: Independently published

Copyright @2023 by Dr Mariette Jansen

Cover design: Julia Britten JBS Design

All rights are reserved. No part of this publication may be reproduced, stored in a retrieval system or transmitted in any form or by any means, electronic, mechanical, photocopying, recording or otherwise, without the prior written permission of the copyright owner.

Endorsements

'I read Mariette's latest book 'Magical ME' and absolutely loved it. As a matter of fact, I couldn't put it down, I got completely enthralled. The language used in the book is clear and makes you really think about the relationship with yourself and how to improve it.

I like the questions asked and the space in the book for making notes. It is not a book that just tells you what to do; it helps you to put the suggestions into practice. This book is for anyone who want to have the best relationship with oneself.'

Leonie Wright

'I loved the stories to explain clearly what the effect is of not being kind to yourself or the opposite. It is such an easy read and in its simplicity is extremely helpful. I can really feel the benefits of the daily practice and feel much lighter.'

Diana Wilson

'Rightly chosen title about baby steps. I didn't feel overwhelmed or bored, which happens usually when I pick up a self-help book. Highly recommend this one.'

Clare Wilson

'I love how simple the book reads, yet so insightful. It offers such uncomplicated steps to improving the relationship with myself and is easy to read and relate to.'

Chloe Burrell

'Fascinating how often I am unkind to myself without realising. Mariette makes it easy to recognise the patterns that don't serve me. Her writing style makes me feel she is talking directly to me and knows me inside out. A gem of a book for anyone who wants to learn more about themselves. In an easy and entertaining manner. Who wouldn't?'

Alison Walker

Table of Contents

Endorsements V

General Introduction to the Philosophy of Baby Steps 1

Introduction Baby steps Magical ME 11

Section 1: Awareness 17

    Chapter 1: No Judgement 19

    Chapter 2: Taking Stock 27

    Chapter 3: Self-Criticism 31

    Chapter 4: Comparing to Others 35

    Chapter 5: Other People are More Important 43

    Chapter 6: I Beat Myself Up 47

    Chapter 7: Perfectionism 53

    Chapter 8: Can't Say No 57

    Chapter 9: I Doubt My Decisions 61

    Chapter 10: High Expectations 65

    Chapter 11: What Will Others Think? 69

    Chapter 12: Rumination 73

    Chapter 13: Summary Awareness 79

Section 2: Daily Practice 85

   Chapter 14: Benefits of the Magical ME Practice 87

   Chapter 15: Gratitude 91

   Chapter 16: Self-Love and Appreciation 95

   Chapter 17: An Open Mind 99

   Chapter 18: Daily Practice 105

   Chapter 19: Taking Stock Again 207

Epilogue 211

General Introduction to the Philosophy of Baby Steps

I have read zillions of self-help books, educational blogs and watched numerous videos on 'how to', and listened to wonderful podcasts, trying to answer 'how to's', but none of them really helped me. Even though creative solutions were offered, they seemed to be too difficult to act on.

A few examples of what didn't work for me:

- Feeling lonely? Get a dog.

- Suffering from SAD (Seasonal Affective Disorder)? Go on holiday.

- Drinking too much? Join AA.

- Feeling low? Train yourself to be grateful.

- Feeling unfulfilled? Find your purpose.

- Feeling negative? Be positive.

What really helped me was the recognition of the importance of baby steps and celebrating every move forward. It is the 'devil in the detail': the little steps that lead to the finish line of the marathon, the extra 2 pumps in the series of 10 that builds the muscle, a glass of water at the start of the day to lose weight, the one-minute-meditation that stops the outbursts of anger and gives peace of mind ...

You get the zest.

Baby steps are the stepping stones to where you want to be, they give joy, are easy and when you are focused and consistent, those steps will bring you to your destination.

1. Basic components: mindset and behaviour

New behaviour can lead to a healthier and happier you.

But behaviour needs to be supported by the right mindset in order to keep it going.

Anthony's approach

Anthony Robbins is the billion-dollar coach who gets thousands of people into a huge venue for 4 days at the price of several thousands. You get a lot of Anthony for that money. He will start talking and shouting at you from early morning till late at night. And he will make you understand that you can choose your mindset, do whatever you want and achieve your dreams. When you are released after 4 days, you are convinced you can make it happen.

After all, you walked over hot coals, ate wheatgrass, can't bear eating meat anymore, believe in yourself and are glowing with confidence. Because Anthony made you shout out loud: 'I can do it. I am amazing.'

You are motivated to implement new behaviour, but over time nearly everyone who was with you at that seminar will have fallen back into their familiar old behaviour.

Including you.

The changes didn't stick. It was too much in too short a time.

Mariette's approach

Where Anthony shouts you to the top and gets you believing in yourself, he doesn't give you the time and tools to build a solid foundation.

The foundation you need to make the changes stick:

Awareness – how do you get in the way of your happiness and well-being?

Mindset – overcoming resistance to change, committing to it and being consistent.

Discoveries – understanding subconscious automatic pilot behaviour and letting go of those opens up a whole new world.

Processing time – embracing and integrating changes.

Skills – learning the 'how to's' on baby step level.

Understanding and adapting – life is always about you, your unique set of attributes and what is right for you.

Experiences – 'There is a lesson in every experience' (Dr Mariette Jansen) and if you are open to learn, each experience will lead to another one. Very, very exciting.

My philosophy is based on baby steps. Take your time, become (self-) aware, decide on a step, take the step, evaluate, learn and prepare for the next step.

It is about continuously making mini-changes, so your system gets the time to adjust and completely integrate new behaviour and all that goes with it. Such as a mindset. And positive reinforcement.

James Clear, author of 'Atomic Habits', writes about behavioural psychology, habit formation and performance improvements. He came up with the top 5 reasons why the creation of new behaviour and new habits fail. They all focus on effort and looking at effort from a realistic perspective.

1. Too much, too soon: you try to change everything at once

2. Too big: your goal is so big that you get overwhelmed and frustrated because you aren't making progress or you can't notice the progress

3. Result orientated: it is more important to establish a ritual of actions, which will logically lead to the result.
4. Environmental unawareness: you can't change your environment, but what if your behaviour is a response to your environment? Then you have to consider alternative options.
5. Small changes are overlooked and not celebrated enough.

A personal example

I was determined to make changes around 'stuff' in the house. I am not a domestic goddess and find it really hard to have an organized and neat environment.

My option is to go for an instant result or a mindset change. The difference between the two is that the end result of an intense few days of decluttering will look awesome and then the house will quickly return back to the current state.

I knew if I wanted to make a fundamental change, one that involved mindset, new habits and a number of positive experiences, I needed to apply the small changes over time to ultimately create a great long-lasting result.

I set myself a 30 day challenge to say 'Goodbye stuff' in baby steps.

A gentle decluttering process.

I started with my make-up, followed by a tiny cabinet. I did one kitchen drawer, the next day I focused on socks, then handbags. And just 10 minutes a day.

This is the way to create a change in behaviour and mindset.

And it works.

Recently, I was shopping in Costco and I saw sport socks everywhere. I caught myself thinking 'You can never have enough socks', but actually having gone through the process of decluttering, I know I only need 10 pairs of socks and therefore I didn't buy any. I realized I didn't need them and I didn't want them.

This is the journey of creating a foundation of new behaviour and a mindset, which will support me for the rest of my life.

2. Life changes

Making changes is about a process.

For real change to take place, you need to understand what happens, embrace it and make it your mind set.

Anthony is pushing you and helping you to have great experiences, like walking on fire, but he doesn't allow you time to learn how to do it by yourself and in your own way.

And that is why you can't hold onto what you learned that weekend.

He brings you to the top, but you haven't learned the steps to get there. And once you fall down, you will find yourself at the bottom of the mountain, without the skills to climb up again.

3. The magic

The mountaineer who is looking at the summit will never get there.

As on the way he will trip over rocks or holes in the road, that he couldn't see because his focus was on the top.

Had he set out with the focus on only getting through the next metres, he would step by step get closer and possibly reach the summit by surprise.

And during the whole process he would have felt in control by concentrating on his baby steps.

Tips to make changes that last:

- Make your goal a process rather than a result.

    Learning a process means you will never 'arrive', but always ready to apply skills and create experiences. You know if you go through the motions, you will ultimately get to where you want to be. And then you might decide to travel even further...

- Take your time to thoroughly go through each step.

    Embrace the experience of applying new skills, developing your capabilities and creating a deeper understanding of what you are doing. Maybe the way you originally thought it would work, actually doesn't. Maybe you need to personalise the motions to make them more suitable.

- Keep going, never give up.

    'A winner never gives up.' However, if you give yourself a break from baby steps, it is easy to pick up again.

- Notice the changes in behaviour, thoughts and feelings.

    Be aware of what happens to you. Observe and ideally, make notes about your journey. It will help to establish a strong connection with your process and this feeds your motivation and mindset.

- Enjoy the journey.

    Joy is one of the pillars of sustainable change. As Deepak Chopra says in his book about 'The Seven Spiritual Laws Of Success', the law of least effort is all about the joy in doing something that is natural to you. And if it is not natural, like decluttering is to me, you have to find a way to make it work. You don't have to estrange yourself from yourself, you have to find the path to yourself and your way.

4. The series

Happiness is hard work.

Don't expect to be happy, stress free, forever happy in a relationship, okay in a job, or being healthy without putting in work. There is effort involved: learning new skills and of course, apply them and always be ready to deal with the inevitable, change.

In this series of 'Improve Your Life In Baby Steps', the following subjects are covered, at this moment in time, in no particular order:

- Magical ME – Build A Healthy Relationship With Yourself
- Magical WORDS – Become A Better Communicator
- Magical US – Create Healthy Relationships
- Magical CONFIDENCE – Be Grounded And Have Self-Esteem
- Magical SPACE- Cut Clutter In Mind And Life
- Magical CALM – Defy Stress And Anxiety

Each guide is offering information and practical guidance in baby bites, making it easy to make mega changes with minimum effort.

Life is challenging enough as it is.

Introduction Baby steps Magical ME

No one can survive without other people. When we are babies, we need to be looked after and cared for. When we are growing up we need others to connect with, learn from and love. Humans are social animals.

Ed Stafford, a professional survivor, stipulated his biggest challenge in surviving on a deserted island for 60 days ('Naked and Marooned' Netflix series) the lack of human interaction.

It is no wonder then that we are focussed on others. We need them to 'survive' and build a happy life.

Other people and interacting with them are crucial for our survival.

BUT, most people forget who is their forever companion, the most important person in the universe. The one and only to build a beautiful relationship with, because they are with you from birth until the final moment.

That person is YOU.

That person is often forgotten, doesn't get the attention and appreciation it is worthy of.

The person you need to look after and be kind to most of all you, yourself, your beautiful and magical ME.

In the Western World it is promoted that other people are more important than yourself. You have to be kind to others, be nice and accommodating and never consider if it takes too much out of you. If you were to do that, you would be called selfish.

And being selfish is bad.

The definition of selfish according to the Oxford Language Dictionary is 'lacking consideration for other people; concerned mainly with one's own personal profit or pleasure'.

The definition of selfish according to me is 'focussing on self-care, in order to be in the best possible place to serve others'.

The Oxford definition is painting the picture of a person that doesn't care about others, but focuses on their own benefits. My definition is approving of focus on oneself, with the aim to benefit others.

In this book the word 'selfish' is used according to my definition and considered a positive attitude.

Affirmation: 'It is important to be selfish'.

Most of us are familiar with the message that gets communicated on every flight: 'Put your oxygen mask on first, before you help others'. Get yourself in a good place, from where it is so much easier to support others.

If you don't do that, you will hollow yourself out and end up in a place where you are the one who is unhappy and needs support from others because you have a breakdown or get otherwise ill.

It is important to give yourself what you need, so you are strong enough to be there for others.

The negative connotation of selfish often leads to a total disregard of the self.

Have a look yourself:

Do you consider the impact of decisions on your own situation?

Are you more focussed on being kind to others then you are to yourself?

Are you willing to go the extra mile for others, but never for you?

Are you more concerned about what others think of you, than actually considering what you think about it?

Is it important to please people?

As you are the only one who travels with you for the duration of the journey called life, wouldn't it be great to have a relationship with yourself, that equals Best Friend Forever (BFF)? After all, you are the only one who really knows yourself, every thought, feeling, memory, nook and cranny.

A good relationship with yourself is the most important building block for an authentic life.

Living in alignment with who you are, creates the space to make decisions that are suiting and serving you.

When your heart is nurtured and your emotional and spiritual needs are met, you will find yourself in a position where you have so much to give. Without paying the price of resentment, disappointment or a break down.

This book is all about offering you the guidance to becoming your own BFF. And understanding how you sabotage yourself.

How do I guide you to become your own BFF?

Let's assume you are not there yet and need to make some changes.

The opportunity to change starts with awareness.

After all, how can you know what isn't right when you don't know?

You are eating sweets because you like them. However, once you have been made aware that sugar is bad for your teeth and your health, you might choose to make a change and stop eating them.

The important awareness is around you and how you treat yourself.

How well do you know yourself and how self-aware are you?

Are you judgmental?

Unkind?

Critical?

The baby step guide to Magical ME has 2 sections.

Section 1 presents you with 10 thoughts of behaviorial patterns that block the blooming of your BFF relationship. It aims to make you aware of what you are doing to yourself. Awareness is the first step to change.

Section 2 is your daily practice. The tool which supports the development of a BFF relationship with yourself. With elements such as gratitude, self-appreciation (which leads to self-love), no judgment and an open mind.

As this guide takes you through a process during a few weeks, it makes sense to use the parts in the book to make notes, so you can observe your changes. If you are good at journaling and need more space than is offered in this book, get yourself a separate notebook.

Section 1
Awareness

Chapter 1
No Judgement

How many of you are continuously judging yourself and your actions?

Labelling yourself or events in life as good or bad doesn't serve a purpose. It stops you to be open minded and inquisitive, it offers a false sense of security, as life is continuously changing and it shows an arrogance, because how could you possibly offer a conclusion if you don't know what is happening next?

The following story by Eckhart Tolle (A New Earth) is a great example of the limitations of judgments.

-0-0-0-

A wise man won an expensive car in a lottery. His family and friends were very happy for him and came to celebrate. 'Isn't it great!' they said. 'You are so lucky.' The man smiled and said 'Is that so?'

For a few weeks he enjoyed driving the car. Then one day a drunken driver crashed into his new car at an intersection and he ended up in the hospital, with multiple injuries. His family and friends came to see him and said, 'That was really unfortunate.' Again, the man smiled and said, 'Is that so?'

While he was in hospital, one night there was a landslide and his house fell into the sea. His friends came the next day, informed him about his house and said, 'Weren't you lucky to have been here in hospital.' The man answered, 'Is that so?'

Judgement is important in practical situations: enough food in the fridge, enough fuel in the tank, etc.

Judgement is needed to plan: how long will it take to walk to the station, to finish this paper, etc.

Judgment helps to keep yourself safe: this area of town feels threatening, this bootcamp is too intense, etc.

But in most other situations, how does judgement support your happiness?

Judgment leads to a dead-end street. The moment where you decide this is good or bad, you stop contemplating and discovering. It might give a sense of security 'to know', but it is a false sense of security.

-0-0-0-

The Difference Between an Observation, Judgement and Opinion

There is a difference between an observation (facts), judgment (wrong or right), and a personal opinion (I like it or not). Understanding the difference between those will be helpful to learn to leave judgment behind.

Situation a.

Situation: a group of four friends has planned a day out to a local Flower Show. A few days before the event one of them, Clare, cancels. Again. She is known for her late withdrawals from group activities.

Reactions:

Obelia one of the three who is going says: 'It is quite normal that Clare cancels. This is the fourth time in a row.'

Jasmin, another of the party go'ers: 'It's ridiculous. She is unreliable and should be planning her life better.'

Oprah, the last one mentions: 'I will miss her. It is a real shame she can't make it.'

Situation b:

The four of them are planning a holiday abroad and have decided on the destination Spain, when Clare brings in new brochures and options about Greece, which is her favourite.

Reactions:

Obelia: 'Clare, we all had Spain in mind up till now. Why don't we stick with it?'

Jasmin: 'Clare, you are ridiculous. It is stupid to start all over and it's wrong to change your mind all of a sudden.'

Oprah: 'I find it hard to change to another country, now I am so set on tapas and white beaches.'

Notice the difference between the three girls and their reactions.

Obelia is observing. She takes everything in, very factual and descriptive. You wouldn't know her personal thoughts about the situation.

Jasmin is quick to point out what is wrong or right about a situation or reaction. Bang in there, black and white. Arrogant as well, pretending to know best.

Oprah is very clear on her point of view. She won't hold back telling you what she thinks about something, but communicates clearly that it is her personal view.

-0-0-0-

What are the Differences Between an Observation, Judgement and Opinion?

An observation refrains from any judgment and describes facts.

A judgment puts you in the position of arrogance and you are either admiring or condemning the other person or their actions.

An opinion is connected with you, you own it as it is about you and how you are affected.

Judgment is the least helpful when you try to build a better relationship with yourself.

$$-0\text{-}0\text{-}0\text{-}$$

Practice

Observe your internal dialogue.

Are you kind and gentle with yourself?

Are you judging yourself?

Is there a pattern?

Whenever you observe yourself judging, try to rephrase the judgment into an observation.

Example:

'How stupid, I was again too late.' Clearly judgmental.

'I noticed I was late again.' Observation.

Then question yourself if you could do something differently next time:

'Next time I will leave earlier.'

Notes / journal

Chapter 2
Taking Stock

It is important to know your current BFF level of the relationship with yourself, so you can measure changes when you have gone through the baby step programme.

Answer the following questions with a number between 0 and 10. Zero means that you don't recognise this situation and 10 means it is overwhelmingly true. The numbers in between indicate the strength of its influence or impact.

		0 - 10
1.	I am critical of myself	
2.	I compare myself to others and feel less good, clever or pretty	
3.	Other people are more important than me	
4.	I beat myself up	
5.	I am a perfectionist	
6.	I can't say no	
7.	I doubt my decisions	
8.	I have high expectations of myself	
9.	I am concerned what other people think of me	
10.	I ruminate	

Well done for answering honestly.

Is there a pattern?

Please don't judge yourself.

If you notice you are judging yourself, don't judge yourself for it.

Write in your notebook about it and rephrase what you are saying to yourself as an observation, facts.

Notes / journal

Chapter 3
Self-Criticism

Do you speak to yourself the same way you speak to others?

Do you speak to others the way you speak to yourself?

I bet, you wouldn't dare.

-0-0-0-

It seems okay for most people to be extremely unkind and critical towards themselves, but if you were to talk to others like you do to yourself, you wouldn't have any friends left.

You are having double standards: what is okay for other people, is not okay for you.

That is unreasonable.

Why would you treat yourself differently than others?

How is being critical helpful?

Several studies have shown that positive feedback helps to build confidence and motivates. Criticism however, depletes energy, demotivates and contributes to a negative self-image.

Every time you are critical of yourself, you deplete your energy, reduce your motivation and feed a negative self-image.

-0-0-0-

Practice

- Observe your internal dialogue.
- List when and how you criticise yourself.
- Write down exactly the words you are using.
- Whose language are you using? Is it yours? Maybe your mothers? Other people?
- Make the conscious decision to stop the self-criticising habit and every time you notice a criticism, pretend you are talking to a friend and rephrase what you originally said as if you are talking to a friend.
- Write about your discoveries and experiences.

Notes / journal

Chapter 4
Comparing to Others

Social comparison theory suggests that you value your own personal and social worth by assessing how you compare to others regarding actions, accomplishments and opinions (Leon Festinger, 1954).

As social animals, we operate in a social environment and are looking to fit in.

And comparison offers a ranking which shows you where you are in the system.

Some psychological reasons behind comparing yourself to others:

1. Social Appraisal

    There seems a natural tendency to evaluate yourself by comparing abilities, traits, achievements, and possessions. This provides a benchmark for self-assessment and gives an understanding of your strengths and weaknesses.

2. Self-Esteem

    By comparing yourself to others, you might seek affirmation, coming from the famous need for external validation. If you perceive yourself as better in certain aspects, it will boost your self-esteem. On the other hand, if you observe yourself as less, it leads to feelings of inadequacy and lowered self-esteem.

3. Norms and Standards

    Social comparisons give a sense of what is considered normal or acceptable in a particular context, especially insights into societal standards and expectations. This will influence your choices and behaviour.

4. Goal Setting

    Looking at others can act as a motivator for personal growth and goal setting. When you understand how others achieve certain milestones or achievements, it could inspire aspirations.

Social comparison can work in your favour, but often it works negatively. The reason for that is that you can only compare what you see at the service. Like the unknown athlete, who wins gold out of the blue and sparks some jealousy. However, they have been dedicating their life, diet and career 12 hours a day to their sports. Who would be jealous of that?

Or social media…. Where an 'Insta-life' is glamorous and happy, but real life is an unhappy affair. The comparison doesn't represent reality.

Comparing to Others

Do you notice yourself comparing yourself with others regularly? It is highly likely that it means that your value is determined by others. You either feel better because you compare with people who you perceive as less, or you feel low because you notice that so many people have more fun and success. The psychological impact of this is that you feed your insecurity, take away joy, maybe spark jealousy and in general feel a deep sense of being 'not good enough'.

You are working on becoming BFF with yourself. In that journey is no place for the comparison with others. You are connecting with the you inside, that offers what you have to work with. Accepting you, finding your voice, deciding what makes you happy and not caring what other people do.

You might be less successful than a friend. Does that make you less valuable?

Your financial situation could be better. Would that effect the relationship with yourself?

The moment you allow others to determine how you feel about yourself, you have lost yourself.

-0-0-0-

'I Shouldn't Be Here; It Shouldn't be Like This and I Don't Want It!

It sounds like a temper tantrum, fitting a 3 year old. Screaming in the aisle in the supermarket, letting the whole world know that life isn't fair. Jill was having a tantrum like this regularly. She was so pissed off with all that didn't go her way.

Her friends had brilliant careers. After uni, Jill chose to go travelling but most of her friends couldn't wait to climb the corporate ladder, which they did fast and furious with great success. And good bonuses. And flats in the city.

Jill hadn't found her feet yet in the working world. She was a PA to a SEO of an impressive company, but compared to her friends, she felt it was nothing.

Other friends had babies. And a house in the suburbs. Married to a solid partner. They had focus and purpose. Jill was single. Her only romances were hopeless internet dates and disappointing one night stands.

Why Couldn't She Have What the Others Had?

Jill made herself unhappy by focusing on comparing herself with her friends. Their Instagram lives looked so much more exciting than hers…. They had money, purpose, beautiful relationships and lived Walt Disney lives.

Jill was so busy looking at her friends, that she lost total view of all she had: independence, freedom to do whatever she liked and less responsibilities.

She also only glimpsed the surface of their lives. The frustration at work, Imposter Syndromes, sleepless nights because of work or babies, in-laws and their expectations and potentially a lot of unfulfillment and unhappiness.

The Unhelpful Questions and Remarks That Arise When Comparing:

- What is wrong with me?
- I should be in a better place.
- I have lost so much time….
- Why am I so unlucky?

Why Comparing is Harmful and Triggering You to Feel Low

The subjects you compare to are usually people you think are in a better position. That will make you feel inferior or incompetent.

Most people share the shiny shield that hides the darkness. You never see their real lives.

Comparing leads to frustration and lowers confidence.

You have your life to live. Not that of others. Focussing on others distracts you from yourself.

$$-0-0-0-$$

Practice

Notice when you are on social media if and how you are comparing yourself to others.

How does it affect how you feel about yourself?

Is this helpful for an authentic relationship with you?

Experiment with spending less time on social media and how that affects how you think about yourself.

Notes / journal

Chapter 5
Other People are More Important

This is one of the biggest bug bears and unhealthy statements ever.

How can you make the relationship with yourself beautiful and supportive if you believe that other people are more important than you are?

-0-0-0-

It Isn't Selfish to Prioritise Yourself. It Is Selfish Not To.

Because if you are not in a good place, always running after others, making sure they are okay at your detriment, you will reach the stage where you need to be looked after. Or you have become sour and resentful and have a negative affect on others.

For a lot of people this statement is ingrained from an early age by parents and carers. It just suited them better if you tuned into them and other adults. They would tell you to be kind, to do things, to serve and to put yourself last. You have taken it on board and never ever thought about it properly.

Until now.

If you make yourself more important than others, you will be able to become the best happy version of yourself and give others what they need to the best of your ability.

You can choose sometimes to make another person a priority. Because they are in a bad place and need your attention and care. But that should always be a conscious decision and ideally with boundaries.

How many opportunities in life have you missed because you made yourself unimportant and gave the lead to others?

Examples:

How often did you take a shift you didn't want to help someone out?

Did you go to work while ill, because you didn't want to burden your colleagues?

How many times did you step back to make space for others?

-0-0-0-

Practice

List situations that were informed by the idea that others are more important than you.

How have you been positively affected by these?

How have you been negatively affected by these?

What would your BFF have liked you to do?

When you are in a situation, can you start choosing yourself over others?

Notes / journal

Chapter 6
I Beat Myself Up

It's a classic display of not loving and accepting yourself.

How would it be to swap the rod for a smile?

How would that affect your relationship with you?

$$-0-0-0-$$

I failed. Again, again and again.

- I came back from the country side, having brought my DS (Darling Son) to a rugby training. It was dark and all of a sudden I found myself on the wrong highway. I had missed the exit. Again.

- I made a coffee and spat it out. Yak. Forgot to put a capsule in the machine. Again.

- When saying goodbye to my other DS at his new university, I dropped a bottle. Full of wine. Oops.

- I made a double booking and had to miss that workshop. Oops.

- I got a message from DS with the request to top-up his lunch account. Forgotten. Again.

- I lost my favourite t-shirt. Damn.
- I lost my favourite jeans. Damn.
- I lost my favourite knickers. Damn.
- I overdid it in the gym. Again.
- I put my coffee (a nice one) in the freezer. Again.
- I got smudges on my white trousers. Again.
- I forgot to buy leeks for the chicken and leek pie. Again.
- And this morning, instead of attending a Speed Awareness Course, I am writing at home, as I didn't have the right ID on me. Oops.

Not too clever, organized and on top of life, I would say.

But it doesn't bother me. Anymore.

Because I have decided that all these little incidents are not important for my level of happiness.

They actually contribute to it as they make me smile and laugh at myself. They give me energy and like this morning, it gave me extra time. All of a sudden, thanks to my mistake, I had a morning free to write and catch up with admin. That's a bonus.

'It is not what happens to you, it is how you react to it that matters' - Epictetus

And especially if it is about little things you do 'wrong', it is easy to beat yourself up and be critical. But what does it give you? Most likely feeling incompetent or annoyed. Is that helpful? And it gets in the way of that smile and that shrug of your shoulders, where you gently let it all fall away.

-0-0-0-

Practice

Observe and write down what you are saying to yourself: 'I am ridiculous', or 'I am an idiot, or other ways you are being critical and judgemental of yourself.

Or telling yourself 'I could never do that', 'I am not good enough', 'other people are much better than me'.

This putting down and telling off is a habit, which is can be changed. The exercise below will take your brain away from the habitual response. You don't have to do anything else but observing and noticing.

The exercise can have different forms:

1. Get a set of square little notes, fold them into smaller squares and tear a piece off or in, every time you notice your unhelpful thought. At the end of each day note down the number of tears.
2. Get a little notebook or use an index card and mark every time the thought appears.
3. At the end of the day, count the totals.
4. At the end of the week, notice how the number of times you beat yourself up has gone done.

It is miraculous how the brain is trained this way. It knows it is not a helpful thought and after training, it will stop that thought to pop up.

Notes / journal

Chapter 7
Perfectionism

Perfectionism is an expression of insecurity. If it is perfect, no one can criticise you. But it takes a lot of time and energy and causes a lot of stress to create that picture perfect.

-0-0-0-

The Price for Perfectionism

I used to dream of being that perfect lady, wearing a red suit and insanely high heels. Feeling in total control and in charge of my life.

Imagine if that had happened?

I would have been so:

- Stressed – continuously on alert to make sure I was doing the right thing and wearing the right red

- Boring – as it would be too risky to be adventurous

- Frustrated – because most of the time I would not manage to be perfect

- Tired – as it would take sooooo much energy to keep the perfectionism going

- Narrow-minded – as I have decided what it means to be perfect, there is no need to be open to other ideas
- Controlling – everything and everybody around me has to behave in a certain way to ensure that I can maintain my perfect state
- Obsessive – my main thing is to be perfect, I can't let go
- And above all, I would be very unhappy and not feeling alive.

So, what's the point?

Perfectionists are inflexible in their observation. Things are black or white, perfect or imperfect. However, if you as a perfectionist change the perception of yourself and become more loving and kinder, it will become easier to deal with non-perfect situations. 'Give yourself some slack' and step out of the drama and the dream / nightmare of perfectionism.

-0-0-0-

Practice

Questions to help you decide if you want to be perfect.

Apply these to different situations.

1. What would it give you to be perfect?
2. What would be your reward for being perfect?
3. Are there other ways you can get those rewards?
4. How much time and effort does it take to be perfect?
5. Is it worth it?

Notes / journal

Chapter 8
Can't Say No

Are you part of the army of people pleasers? Smiling and nodding before you have even heard a request, but overly keen to offer your services?

-0-0-0-

If Only Ursula Could Do It

Ursula felt out of control of her life. She found herself doing things she didn't want to do. She was always busy for others and didn't even have time to think about what it was she wanted. She felt guilty if she didn't help out, bad if something went wrong, even though she couldn't help it, and very overwhelmed and exhausted.

She said to me: 'If only I could say no'.

I smiled and said to her: 'You just said it, didn't you?'

Of course, we both know she said the word with her mouth, but her heart wasn't in it.

Ursula is not alone. A lot of people struggle with saying no. And changing that is not easy, because there are usually deep-rooted ideas and beliefs preventing to consider the option of saying no.

But is learning to say NO the solution?

Lots of people think so.

I don't.

I think you have to learn to say a proper yes. A proper 'yes' is a response to a request that you have considered seriously, which is reflecting your conscious decision to go ahead. Knowing you can manage the request and being aware of the consequences.

In the moment, saying yes will make everybody happy, but there is a price to pay.

Learning to say yes full-heartedly, aware of the after-effects and committed to stick to your promise, is the way forward. If you can do that, you are clear in your communication, willingness and expectations. The energy of your yes is unambiguous and honest.

In the moment, saying yes from a place of fear because you 'can't say no' carries the energy of frustration, ambiguity and passive acceptance. It leaves you feeling disempowered and not feeling good about yourself.

If you can't say a full yes straight away, there is no need to say no.

It is as simple as being genuine: you would love to say yes, but you want to check out if you can do it, or discuss with somebody else and you will get back to the person with a clear answer at a defined moment in the future, which can be an hour later, a day or a week.

$$-0\text{-}0\text{-}0\text{-}$$

Practice:

From now on, when someone asks you a favour, don't go auto-pilot yes, but ask for more time as your standard answer. Then take yourself through the following sequence 'the 6 magic questions' for the 'yes' and the 'no' answer:

1. What does it give me (positives)?
2. What does it take from me (negatives)?
3. Who benefits?
4. Who pays the price?
5. Is it important?
6. Is it my responsibility?

This will present you with a good picture of the consequences of either answer, and will make it possible to make an informed choice.

Notes / journal

Chapter 9
I Doubt My Decisions

People who struggle with decisions are often so insecure that any decision needs to be validated upfront by others: 'What do you think I should do?' Following a decision, there is still doubt because there is no internal confirmation. This is combined with fear for negative feedback.

-0-0-0-

Jan could not make decisions. Because any decision was a statement and a statement could be criticised. So, rather than making a decision, she refrained from them.

Which, by the way, is also a decision. But, it gives a sense of safety as there is always the excuse that you are in the process of making a decision.

Jan was a very outgoing personality, had lots of friends and came across as a confident and fun woman. But she carried a heavy burden under her light-heartedness. She was very insecure and could not handle negative comments about herself or her behaviour. As a consequence, she found it extremely difficult to make choices and decisions.

It was one of the things we worked on and one day she called me out of the blue, almost shouting through the phone: 'I did it. I bought a whole set of suitcases, within 10 minutes and I am really happy with them'.

Buying a set of suitcases sounds such a trivial action, but for Jan it represented how she had changed and how her confidence had grown. She wasn't bothered about making a wrong decision anymore. She stood in her power, purchased what she liked and with her developed 'internal frame of reference' she was happy with her choice. That was all that mattered.

In times before she displayed an 'external frame of reference', which meant that it was more important to her what others thought of her decisions than she did herself. She was feeding her low confidence and self-esteem.

-0-0-0-

Practice:

Discover what is affecting your decision-making confidence.

Questions Series 1

1. Do you value other people's opinions more than your own?
2. Are you quick to think 'I got it wrong'?

3. Do you go 'with the flow' and easily adapt to others wishes?
4. Are you often changing your mind?
5. Can you hear yourself say 'I am not sure' a lot?
6. Do you find it hard to make choices?

Questions Series 2

1. Do you value your own opinion?
2. Are you open to other people's opinions, without straight away thinking that they are right?
3. Do you think through your opinions?
4. Are you open to change your mind?
5. Can you hear yourself say 'I am right' a lot?
6. Do you find it easy to make choices?

The first series of questions are indicating your external frame of reference, the second are about an internal frame of reference.

If you score for an external frame of reference, could you start making changes?

Notes / journal

Chapter 10
High Expectations

Expectations and disappointments go hand in hand.

High expectations? They will lead to massive disappointments, as you will definitely fail at meeting all of them.

-0-0-0-

Dian was your typical striver, all the time. And why not? What is wrong with going for the highest achievable level? It all depends on the price she pays for it.

Dian is a project manager and she wants to deliver within the deadline. Her bosses love her for that. Her team members less so as she can be quite bullying and putting them under pressure. Dian has sleepless nights when deadlines get closer.

Part of the delivery timings are out of her hands. During a project there are always unexpected situations, events and changes. No one can be blamed for that. It is just life. But not for Dian. She makes herself responsible for every element and especially when things go 'wrong' she gets extremely stressed.

Dian is not helping herself by aiming for such high standards. It makes her less flexible and she perceives changes as mistakes and they are a big deal in her life.

What makes those mistakes a big deal?

- The time afterwards, when she is ruminating and telling herself it is unacceptable.

- The fact she messed up, as in not delivering up to high expectations. But Dian doesn't realise that her unhappiness and dissatisfaction are created by herself.

- The mistake itself and its impact is blown out of proportions and made very important, where most of the times it isn't important or can be rectified easily.

- Punishment in the way of telling herself off follows: 'I screwed up', 'I am useless' and she is feeling angry and frustrated.

There is a potential variety of reasons that Dian sets herself over-the-top high expectations, such as Imposter Syndrome, masking insecurity, the aftermath of narcissistic abuse, low self-esteem or lack of self-appreciation. These are all emotional causes, that stop her loving and appreciating herself.

In order to deal differently with expectations and mistakes Dian needs to step into her head and approach the situation from a rational perspective.

-0-0-0-

Practice:

It is easy to get sucked in by your expectations. What do you expect of yourself? Would you think that to be a reasonable expectation to have of a friend? If not, turn it down.

Treat yourself the way you would treat your friend, to ultimately become your own BFF.

Notes / journal

Chapter 11
What Will Others Think?

One of my favorite sayings is: 'It is none of your business what others think of you.' Everyone is entitled to their opinion, which means that there are thousands of different opinions around. And surely, lots of people will have different thoughts about you. But you know what? That is all out of your control. And relatively unimportant. The main thing is that you know what you think of yourself.

-0-0-0-

Yvonne was always keen to make a good impression. Basically, she was so keen that she was nervous before she went out. Umming and ahing about what to wear. Was it the right thing for the occasion, did her bum look big in it, was the colour okay? It was always difficult to make a decision. Often, she changed a few times before she left the house. And never felt okay with her choice unless someone commented on it.

Recently she wanted to buy a new dress. The lady in the shop said it really flattered her. And another lady, who happened to be there, also commented how lovely she looked in it. So she bought it. If both of them thought it was a good one, it had to be a good one.

She wore the dress to a function at work and got a few compliments. She was absolutely over the moon. Then she wore it to a friend's party and nobody said anything. She was totally in bits.

Yvonne's insecurity around other people could spoil her outings. She was in need of positive confirmation in order to feel good. And if she didn't get that, she felt very low and insignificant.

It is important for Yvonne to do (or wear) the right thing and she is looking continuously for positive feedback and affirmation, believing that others know better than her.

Are you like Yvonne? Aiming to please others and acting in a way that they will approve of? It means that you are neglecting your own opinions and maybe even your own values. You are walking on egg shells and nervous about feedback.

-0-0-0-

Practice:

Observe when you ask yourself the question: 'What will they think?' and change it into 'What do I really think if I was 'alone in the world' and nobody could comment?'

Add questions such as:

- Do I really like this?
- Does it feel good?
- Do I feel a resistance?
- Does it make me smile?

Then come to a conclusion and don't allow yourself to think about it anymore.

Notes / journal

Chapter 12
Rumination

Rumination involves repetitive thinking or dwelling on negative feelings, events, causes and consequences. It is as if your thoughts are running around in a hamster wheel, making you feel more and more stressed. Stress is connected with fear and fear and love don't go together. If you fill yourself with fear, there is no space for love. And in order to be your BFF, you need the love to thrive.

-0-0-0-

If Your Thoughts Were Dollars……

What would you do with 350.000 dollars? Would you buy a house, a car, a holiday, a mink coat or all of these? Would you choose things that you really like or would you buy a shed in a ropy place, a car of a make you dislike, go on a holiday to the Norwegian fjords while you love the beach and buy that mink coat while you hate fur? Of course, you wouldn't. You would spend your money only on things you really love.

Let's make a link to your thoughts. You have at least 50.000 thoughts a day, 350.000 a week. What do you spend your thoughts on? Your father, who you hate, your boss, who you despise, the friend who betrayed you, the mountain of debts that is building up, your insecurity, the diet you are currently doing and frustrated about? Wouldn't you want to spend your mental energy only on things you really love?

Mike Dooley, a spiritual teacher, talks about how thoughts become things. So, you better choose the good ones! Dr Wayne Dyer mentions how thoughts reflects your intentions and in The Secret (the law of attraction) it is pointed out that what you think of, you will attract.

If you consider your thoughts as valuable as your dollars, it makes sense to use them in a positive way, to increase your well-being and attract what you want in life.

-0-0-0-

Practice:

I call this practice 'Stop Spaghetti Thinking'.

When you notice you are ruminating, there is a lot of mental activity. The thought energy is high, but lacks any structure. It is chaotic, repetitive and unhelpful. Like a plate of spaghetti, which you won't be able to eat neatly.

Even though it might feel very busy in your head, you will not have too many different thoughts.

Rumination

This practice if helping to become aware of the main thoughts and how you can respond to them in order to stop the chaos.

Step 1: List your thoughts

Step 2: Finish your thoughts

The concept of Unfinished Business is that thoughts which don't come to a conclusion keep on coming back and they easily become Spaghetti. An example: 'What shall I do on Saturday? I can do x, y, z and more. I don't know what to do.' The thought will keep on coming back and you will add in more and more chaos and drama, until you have changed the Unfinished Business into Finished Business through coming to a conclusion. A conclusion can be the decision to do x, y or z, but it could also be the decision to think about it on Friday and to let it rest until then.

The process is based on the returning question 'What if?'

Repeating the question takes the drama and unclarity away and will cut the spaghetti thoughts in bite size pieces.

What shall I do on Saturday? I have 3 options.

1. What if I choose to do x? It will take a lot of time.
2. What if it takes too much time? I wouldn't be able to go out later.

3. What if I can't go out later? I might miss out.
4. What if I miss out? My friends might not be happy.
5. What if my friends are not happy? They would ditch me.
6. What if they ditched me? They are not real friends then.
7. Conclusion: there is one consequence of choosing x and that is that I won't see my friends.

Then do a similar 'What if' sequence for y and z.

You end up with 3 conclusions and hopefully are able to make a choice.

If not, your decision could be to wait until Friday to make the decision.

Either way, you have cut the Spaghetti into bitesize pieces and can let it rest.

Notes / journal

Chapter 13
Summary Awareness

Well done. You made it to the end of section 1.

The aim of this section is to make you more aware of your authentic traits, underlying subconscious limiting beliefs and learned behaviour that attributes to the relationship with yourself.

Authentic Traits

These are inherent characteristics, qualities and tendencies that are unique to you. They include aspects of your personality, temperament, talents, strengths, and values. Authentic traits play a significant role in shaping your thoughts, actions, and choices.

Limiting Beliefs

Those are beliefs you are not aware of, which hinder your personal development, limit your potential and are restrictive. They come for authority figures in your past, societal conditioning or experiences. Examples are: 'A woman's most important role in life is to be a good mother and wife.' Or 'I am stupid'. Or 'I will never be able to do that'. Limiting beliefs become 'noise on the line' of the authentic you.

Learned Behaviour

This includes both conscious and subconscious patterns of thinking and acting. When you think 'this is how I am', you might often refer to behaviour, which has nothing to do with who you are.

You have learned to behave in ways that make your life easier (If I give in, we won't have an argument), to survive (If I want to be part of this group / family, this is how I need to behave) or to improve your life (Copying the popular person).

While learned behaviour can be valuable, it also contributes to habits that are not aligned with your authentic self or serve your happiness and well-being.

'As soon as we try to inspire other people, or try to say what we think others want to hear or be who we think they want us to be, then we are no longer being authentic. We are coming from the head and not the heart. When we come from the heart instead, we allow the message to come through us, rather than from us.

—Anita Moorjani

Change in Awareness?

Let's check if you have already made changes, thanks to the awareness practices. Answer the following questions with a number between 0 and 10. Zero means that you don't recognise this situation and 10 means it is overwhelmingly true. The numbers in between indicate the strength of its influence or impact.

There is no judgement.

It just is what it is.

		0 - 10
1.	I am critical of myself	
2.	I compare myself to others and feel less good, clever or pretty	
3.	Other people are more important than me	
4.	I beat myself up	
5.	I am a perfectionist	
6.	I can't say no	
7.	I doubt my decisions	
8.	I have high expectations of myself	
9.	I am concerned what other people think of me	
10.	I ruminate	

Practices and Thoughts to Remember:

No judgment

An open mind

Is this helpful?

Am I applying an internal or external frame of reference?

The magic 6 questions sequence

The Spaghetti Exercise

Notes / journal

Section 2
Daily Practice

Chapter 14
Benefits of the Magical ME Practice

Hey there, magical you! The daily practice that I will introduce here, will help you to become even more magical and appreciate the magic of life and yourself, which is presented to you every single day. It will open your eyes to it by some very easy and simple exercises, which hopefully become a habit.

You are more aware which behaviour or thought pattern are getting in the way of valuing yourself. Another thing you might be noticing is that you are more affected by negative than positive and easily forget the good 'stuff'.

The daily practice I am introducing here is aimed to connect with the magical you and developing that important BFF relationship. It is about the gifts of life, your own power, observation, appreciation, gratitude, self-love, discoveries and learning. You will change your mindset, one of the key-elements in becoming your own BFF, and increase your happiness.

Thoughts become things, so choose the good ones, as Mike Dooley, a spiritual teacher, says and by focussing at the end of each day on the good ones, you will go to sleep with them and wake up in a positive mindset, rather than a gloomy one.

Butterfly

The 'Magical Me' practice is built around the symbolism of the butterfly. Most cultures see the butterfly as a symbol for bliss, joy and change.

But butterflies are also very strong and resilient:

- Butterflies are extremely adaptable to their environment and climatic conditions – adaptability and resilience is helpful for happiness.

- Butterflies are always on the move, exploring the world – broadening your horizon and creating new experiences as food for growth.

- The skeleton provides an armour of self-protection – if you create your own safe space, based on self-love and appreciation, you are protected against external negativity.

- The small size keeps their demands small – the less attached you are to 'stuff' the happier you will be.

- Butterflies undergo multiple changes (metamorphosis) to facilitate and carry on life – you will go through multiple, natural and challenging changes supporting your growth when you go with it and creating unhappiness when you resist them.

Notes / journal

Chapter 15
Gratitude

'If you've forgotten the language of gratitude, you'll never be on speaking terms with happiness.'

The simple act of feeling (!) grateful and expressing it has a strong impact on health, well-being and relationships.

A series of recent studies have found positive effects on physical and emotional health.

But.......... it is not about saying or thinking the 'thank you' on automatic pilot. What is essential is the emotion that goes with it. A deeply felt gratitude is what will benefit us. Just automatically blurring out the 'thanks' won't have the same effect as paying conscious attention to the emotion when expressing it.

The scientific gratitude hero is professor Robert Emmons, who has proven that gratefulness inspires happiness.

In one study (conducted by Robert Emmons - University of California – and Mike McCullough - University of Miami), randomly assigned participants were given one of three tasks. Each week, participants kept a short journal. One group briefly described five things they were grateful for that had occurred in the past week, another five recorded daily hassles from the previous week that displeased them, and the neutral group was asked to list five events or circumstances that affected them, but they were not told whether to focus on the positive or on the negative. Ten weeks later, participants in the gratitude group felt better about their lives as a whole and were a full 25 percent happier than the hassled group. They reported fewer health complaints and also did more exercise per week.

In a later study by Emmons, people were asked to write every day about things for which they were grateful. The daily practice led to greater increases in gratitude than the weekly journaling in the first study. And there was another benefit: participants in the gratitude group also reported offering others more emotional support or help with a personal problem.

Conclusion: notice what to be thankful for, feel it, express it, become healthier and happier and feel able to help others.

Notes / journal

Chapter 16
Self-Love and Appreciation

Real love is founded and grounded in self-love'
~ Dr Mariette Jansen

When I accept myself, I am freed from the burden of needing you to accept me'
~ Dr Steve Maraboli

If you know yourself, the good, the bad and the ugly, you can start to accept who you are - exactly as you are. It can feel like a challenge to accept without judgment some aspects of your character that you don't perceive as positive, such as laziness.

However, if that is part of you, it is important to honour that instead of denying it. It is still there, even if you deny it. Learning to see the benefits of laziness, enjoying it and not letting it work against you will lead you to be able to embrace it as part of who you are, and to, therefore, love it. From love, you can move on to nurturing, to growing, developing, thriving and flourishing.

'Know yourself to improve yourself'
~ Auguste Comte

Love is a word and an emotion we tend to direct to others and definitely not towards ourselves. In most cultures self-love is easily pointed at as selfish, egocentric and WRONG! However, in order to be able to truly give love, you need to be able to give it to yourself. Imagine accepting, loving and enjoying yourself as your BFF. And then sharing that love with others. What is the value of giving away something that you don't value for yourself? Like giving a present that you wouldn't want yourself?

The Magical Me process will help you to conquer the embarrassment by asking you each day to contemplate how valuable you were and express it. This will feed into your skill to detach yourself from your own criticism and judgment and look at yourself through loving eyes.

Notes / journal

Chapter 17
An Open Mind

'The only constant in life is change' - Heraclitus

In order to deal with change effectively, you will have learn continuously.

In order to learn properly, you need an open mind.

-0-0-0-

'I want to go up'. The little voice sounded determined. And the looks went with it. Strong brown eyes. Serious face. Little fists clenched. There was no leeway. The only way was up.

My little Ollie, aged two, was not taking any prisoners. He knew what he wanted and he pestered me for months.

So, what was it he wanted?

We lived in a Victorian house on the outskirts of London. With a loft that was only accessible via a folding loft ladder. One of those that is totally unsuitable for little kiddies. And that was the ladder that Ollie wanted to climb.

As a responsible mum, I said no.

Again and again.

Until I gave in.

The adventure started.

Ollie excited.

Me, apprehensive and careful.

The ladder was down. Ollie started to go up and I was close to him to keep him safe.

My hands close to his chubby legs, in case he missed a step.

Together we climbed to the top, where we had to tackle a funny sidestep to actually arrive at the loft space.

I don't think I said it to him, but I thought: 'There is a lot of crap in the loft, rubbish, dirty stuff we should have got rid of a long time ago. There is nothing of interest.'

But Ollie had a different perspective.

He stood still and looked towards a round window, full of spiderwebs.

The sun shone through it, illuminating half open boxes with things, whatever those things were.

He then looked at me, eyes bright with delight and said with a big smile: 'Awesome.'

I took a deep breath and tried to look at the world through his eyes.

And that was when I saw wonderful things: secrets, hidden in boxes. Some partly revealed in bright colours, others hiding underneath. There was even a bathtub with a dancing ball (the reason the ceiling in the kitchen fell down a few years later, but hey, that has nothing to do with the experience at that moment).

The sun dancing, the spiders moving around.... it was an undiscovered treasure chest.

At that moment I realized how I had closed my mind. How I had forgotten to look at things without anticipation and judgement. How I prevented myself looking at the loft space with fresh eyes. How the practical elements of the loft took over my perception.

And looking at the world like that has given me fantastic experiences, opened my eyes to new perspectives and has been generally enriching.

Three helpful mind processes to support me being open minded:

1. I have no thoughts about this situation / experience, other than curiosity
2. When I notice I anticipate an outcome, I switch that anticipation off
3. I don't judge the process, I just observe

-0-0-0-

'Never Stop Learning, Because Life Never Stops Teaching'

The importance on continuous learning helps you to adapt to change, makes you resilient and equipped for new challenges. Even if it is just remembering something you knew before, which has sunk further into your subconscious.

With an open mind it is easier to make new discoveries and learnings about yourself, others and the world and it is part of your daily Magical ME practice.

Notes / journal

Chapter 18
Daily Practice

A daily practice of just a few minutes is all you need to successfully change your mindset and the relationship with yourself.

If you would like to love yourself more, wish your days to be brighter and want to feel happier, the only thing you have to do for the coming 6 weeks is fill in your daily record.

Keywords are observation, non-judgment, open mind, curiosity, kindness and appreciation.

Nothing complicated.

And each week, you go through the past 7 days and fill in the weekly review.

It's not taking up a lot of time and the results are mind blowing.

How To Go With It?

First of all, read through the different questions, so you know what you are looking out for.

Because you have committed to answer those questions, you subconsciously program your mind to be more alert and notice relevant situations.

The first question is about what you are grateful for. This can be anything from your family to the smile you got from the girl at the cashpoint or the fact you just missed stepping into a dog deposit on the street. Small or big, that is not relevant. What is relevant is that you recognise that something good happened and acknowledge it.

The next question is about what you are proud of or pleased with about yourself. Most people downplay their achievements, and you are highly likely one of them. To get you out of that groove, step back and observe yourself as if you are watching someone else. Can you see how an open mind and a non-judgmental attitude will help to notice? Anything counts. You can be proud of not shouting back, or pleased with the fact you picked somebody else's litter and put that in the bin. Or won a million-dollar client with your proposal.

The third question is helping you to notice what you learned today or that you got a reminder of something that you knew but what had disappeared to the background of your mind. Believe me, every day offers you lessons, if only you can see them.

Then you are asked about what you did differently, in the light of developing that BFF relationship with yourself. Referring to the 10 statements which hinder or support it, this question will challenge you to enter new territory. You might think today about what you want to change tomorrow...

The fifth question encourages you to make your rumination, which is often an automatic reaction, clear and inspires you to take the right action to take control.

And lastly, how do you perceive your happiness level? A number between 1 and 10: 1 is super crap and 10 super duper. This is your perception. But also, find what contributed to it. Once you are very clear about what makes you happy, you can make sure you create more of it.

Interestingly, I had a few days where I scored an 8 but after reflection, I changed that to a 10. It was as if the more challenging elements of the day didn't touch me inside, but were sliding off me like water of a duck. I had built that magical state of being where my inner happiness determined the day. Not external events or other people.

There is no space for journaling, but you have your notebook if you want to journal through your experiences.

After 7 days, you are asked to look through the week and come up with a summary of the week. And after 6 weeks you will be able to write your own conclusions and feeling great!

Daily Mindset Practice Sheet

Day nr: 1 Date: _____

1. What are three things I am grateful for today?

    a. _____

    b. _____

    c. _____

2. What are three things I am pleased with / proud of?

    a. _____

    b. _____

    c. _____

3. What did I learn today or what got confirmed?

    _____

    _____

    _____

    _____

    _____

    _____

    _____

4. What did I do differently today that benefitted the relationship with myself and contributed to BFF?

_____
_____
_____
_____
_____

5. What were my returning unhelpful thoughts and how did I deal with them?

_____
_____
_____
_____

6. What was my happiness level today? (0 – 10) and what was the main contributor?

_____
_____
_____
_____
_____

Daily Mindset Practice Sheet

Day nr: 2   Date: _____

1. What are three things I am grateful for today?

    a. _____

    b. _____

    c. _____

2. What are three things I am pleased with / proud of?

    a. _____

    b. _____

    c. _____

3. What did I learn today or what got confirmed?

    _____

    _____

    _____

    _____

    _____

    _____

    _____

4. What did I do differently today that benefitted the relationship with myself and contributed to BFF?

___

5. What were my returning unhelpful thoughts and how did I deal with them?

___

6. What was my happiness level today? (0 – 10) and what was the main contributor?

___

Magical ME

Daily Mindset Practice Sheet

Day nr: 3   Date: _____

1. What are three things I am grateful for today?

    a. _____

    b. _____

    c. _____

2. What are three things I am pleased with / proud of?

    a. _____

    b. _____

    c. _____

3. What did I learn today or what got confirmed?

    _____

    _____

    _____

    _____

    _____

    _____

    _____

4. What did I do differently today that benefitted the relationship with myself and contributed to BFF?

_____
_____
_____
_____
_____

5. What were my returning unhelpful thoughts and how did I deal with them?

_____
_____
_____
_____

6. What was my happiness level today? (0 – 10) and what was the main contributor?

_____
_____
_____
_____
_____

Daily Mindset Practice Sheet

Day nr: 4   Date: _____

1. What are three things I am grateful for today?

   a. _____

   b. _____

   c. _____

2. What are three things I am pleased with / proud of?

   a. _____

   b. _____

   c. _____

3. What did I learn today or what got confirmed?

   _____

   _____

   _____

   _____

   _____

   _____

4. What did I do differently today that benefitted the relationship with myself and contributed to BFF?

___

5. What were my returning unhelpful thoughts and how did I deal with them?

___

6. What was my happiness level today? (0 – 10) and what was the main contributor?

___

Daily Mindset Practice Sheet

Day nr: 5   Date: _____

1. What are three things I am grateful for today?

    a. _____

    b. _____

    c. _____

2. What are three things I am pleased with / proud of?

    a. _____

    b. _____

    c. _____

3. What did I learn today or what got confirmed?

    _____

    _____

    _____

    _____

    _____

    _____

    _____

4. What did I do differently today that benefitted the relationship with myself and contributed to BFF?

_____

_____

_____

_____

_____

5. What were my returning unhelpful thoughts and how did I deal with them?

_____

_____

_____

_____

6. What was my happiness level today? (0 – 10) and what was the main contributor?

_____

_____

_____

_____

_____

Magical ME

Daily Mindset Practice Sheet

Day nr: 6   Date: _____

1. What are three things I am grateful for today?

    a. _____

    b. _____

    c. _____

2. What are three things I am pleased with / proud of?

    a. _____

    b. _____

    c. _____

3. What did I learn today or what got confirmed?

    _____

    _____

    _____

    _____

    _____

    _____

    _____

4. What did I do differently today that benefitted the relationship with myself and contributed to BFF?

_____
_____
_____
_____
_____

5. What were my returning unhelpful thoughts and how did I deal with them?

_____
_____
_____
_____

6. What was my happiness level today? (0 – 10) and what was the main contributor?

_____
_____
_____
_____
_____

Daily Mindset Practice Sheet

Day nr: 7   Date: _____

1. What are three things I am grateful for today?

    a. _____

    b. _____

    c. _____

2. What are three things I am pleased with / proud of?

    a. _____

    b. _____

    c. _____

3. What did I learn today or what got confirmed?

    _____

    _____

    _____

    _____

    _____

    _____

    _____

4. What did I do differently today that benefitted the relationship with myself and contributed to BFF?

_____
_____
_____
_____
_____

5. What were my returning unhelpful thoughts and how did I deal with them?

_____
_____
_____
_____

6. What was my happiness level today? (0 – 10) and what was the main contributor?

_____
_____
_____
_____
_____

Weekly Mindset Summary Sheet

Week nr: 1   Date: _____

1. What are three things I am grateful for this week?

    a. _____

    b. _____

    c. _____

2. What are three things I am pleased with / proud of??

    a. _____

    b. _____

    c. _____

3. What is my most important learning this week or what got confirmed?

    _____

    _____

    _____

    _____

    _____

    _____

4. What did I do differently today that benefitted the relationship with myself and contributed to BFF?

_____

_____

_____

_____

_____

5. What were my returning unhelpful thoughts this week and what was the most effective way I dealt with them?

_____

_____

_____

_____

6. What was my happiness level this week? (0 – 10) and what was the main contributor?

_____

_____

_____

_____

_____

Daily Mindset Practice Sheet

Day nr: 8   Date: _____

1. What are three things I am grateful for today?

    a. _____

    b. _____

    c. _____

2. What are three things I am pleased with / proud of?

    a. _____

    b. _____

    c. _____

3. What did I learn today or what got confirmed?

    _____

    _____

    _____

    _____

    _____

    _____

    _____

4. What did I do differently today that benefitted the relationship with myself and contributed to BFF?

_____
_____
_____
_____
_____

5. What were my returning unhelpful thoughts and how did I deal with them?

_____
_____
_____
_____

6. What was my happiness level today? (0 – 10) and what was the main contributor?

_____
_____
_____
_____
_____

Daily Mindset Practice Sheet

Day nr: 9	Date: _____

1. What are three things I am grateful for today?

    a. _____

    b. _____

    c. _____

2. What are three things I am pleased with / proud of?

    a. _____

    b. _____

    c. _____

3. What did I learn today or what got confirmed?

    _____

    _____

    _____

    _____

    _____

    _____

    _____

4. What did I do differently today that benefitted the relationship with myself and contributed to BFF?

_____
_____
_____
_____
_____

5. What were my returning unhelpful thoughts and how did I deal with them?

_____
_____
_____
_____

6. What was my happiness level today? (0 – 10) and what was the main contributor?

_____
_____
_____
_____
_____

Magical ME

Daily Mindset Practice Sheet

Day nr: 10 Date: _____

1. What are three things I am grateful for today?

    a. _____

    b. _____

    c. _____

2. What are three things I am pleased with / proud of?

    a. _____

    b. _____

    c. _____

3. What did I learn today or what got confirmed?

    _____
    _____
    _____
    _____
    _____
    _____
    _____

4. What did I do differently today that benefitted the relationship with myself and contributed to BFF?

_____
_____
_____
_____
_____

5. What were my returning unhelpful thoughts and how did I deal with them?

_____
_____
_____
_____

6. What was my happiness level today? (0 – 10) and what was the main contributor?

_____
_____
_____
_____
_____

Daily Mindset Practice Sheet

Day nr: 11   Date: _____

1. What are three things I am grateful for today?

    a. _____

    b. _____

    c. _____

2. What are three things I am pleased with / proud of?

    a. _____

    b. _____

    c. _____

3. What did I learn today or what got confirmed?

    _____

    _____

    _____

    _____

    _____

    _____

4. What did I do differently today that benefitted the relationship with myself and contributed to BFF?

_____
_____
_____
_____
_____

5. What were my returning unhelpful thoughts and how did I deal with them?

_____
_____
_____
_____

6. What was my happiness level today? (0 – 10) and what was the main contributor?

_____
_____
_____
_____
_____

Daily Mindset Practice Sheet

Day nr: 12   Date: _____

1. What are three things I am grateful for today?

    a. _____

    b. _____

    c. _____

2. What are three things I am pleased with / proud of?

    a. _____

    b. _____

    c. _____

3. What did I learn today or what got confirmed?

    _____

    _____

    _____

    _____

    _____

    _____

    _____

4. What did I do differently today that benefitted the relationship with myself and contributed to BFF?

_____
_____
_____
_____
_____

5. What were my returning unhelpful thoughts and how did I deal with them?

_____
_____
_____
_____

6. What was my happiness level today? (0 – 10) and what was the main contributor?

_____
_____
_____
_____
_____

Daily Mindset Practice Sheet

Day nr: 13   Date: _____

1. What are three things I am grateful for today?

    a. _____

    b. _____

    c. _____

2. What are three things I am pleased with / proud of?

    a. _____

    b. _____

    c. _____

3. What did I learn today or what got confirmed?

    _____

    _____

    _____

    _____

    _____

    _____

4. What did I do differently today that benefitted the relationship with myself and contributed to BFF?

_____
_____
_____
_____
_____

5. What were my returning unhelpful thoughts and how did I deal with them?

_____
_____
_____
_____

6. What was my happiness level today? (0 – 10) and what was the main contributor?

_____
_____
_____
_____
_____

Daily Mindset Practice Sheet

Day nr: 14   Date: _____

1. What are three things I am grateful for today?

    a. _____

    b. _____

    c. _____

2. What are three things I am pleased with / proud of?

    a. _____

    b. _____

    c. _____

3. What did I learn today or what got confirmed?

    _____

    _____

    _____

    _____

    _____

    _____

    _____

4. What did I do differently today that benefitted the relationship with myself and contributed to BFF?

_____
_____
_____
_____
_____

5. What were my returning unhelpful thoughts and how did I deal with them?

_____
_____
_____
_____

6. What was my happiness level today? (0 – 10) and what was the main contributor?

_____
_____
_____
_____
_____

Weekly Mindset Summary Sheet

Week nr: 2   Date: _____

1. What are three things I am grateful for this week?

    a. _____

    b. _____

    c. _____

2. What are three things I am pleased with / proud of??

    a. _____

    b. _____

    c. _____

3. What is my most important learning this week or what got confirmed?

    _____

    _____

    _____

    _____

    _____

Daily Practice

4. What did I do differently today that benefitted the relationship with myself and contributed to BFF?

_____
_____
_____
_____
_____

5. What were my returning unhelpful thoughts this week and what was the most effective way I dealt with them?

_____
_____
_____
_____

6. What was my happiness level this week? (0 – 10) and what was the main contributor?

_____
_____
_____
_____
_____

Magical ME

Daily Mindset Practice Sheet

Day nr: 15　　　　　　　　Date: _____

1. What are three things I am grateful for today?

    a. _____

    b. _____

    c. _____

2. What are three things I am pleased with / proud of?

    a. _____

    b. _____

    c. _____

3. What did I learn today or what got confirmed?

    _____

    _____

    _____

    _____

    _____

    _____

    _____

4. What did I do differently today that benefitted the relationship with myself and contributed to BFF?

_____
_____
_____
_____
_____

5. What were my returning unhelpful thoughts and how did I deal with them?

_____
_____
_____
_____

6. What was my happiness level today? (0 – 10) and what was the main contributor?

_____
_____
_____
_____
_____

Daily Mindset Practice Sheet

Day nr: 16   Date: _____

1. What are three things I am grateful for today?

    a. _____

    b. _____

    c. _____

2. What are three things I am pleased with / proud of?

    a. _____

    b. _____

    c. _____

3. What did I learn today or what got confirmed?

    _____
    _____
    _____
    _____
    _____
    _____
    _____

4. What did I do differently today that benefitted the relationship with myself and contributed to BFF?

_____
_____
_____
_____
_____

5. What were my returning unhelpful thoughts and how did I deal with them?

_____
_____
_____
_____

6. What was my happiness level today? (0 – 10) and what was the main contributor?

_____
_____
_____
_____
_____

Daily Mindset Practice Sheet

Day nr: 17   Date: _____

1. What are three things I am grateful for today?

    a. _____

    b. _____

    c. _____

2. What are three things I am pleased with / proud of?

    a. _____

    b. _____

    c. _____

3. What did I learn today or what got confirmed?

    _____

    _____

    _____

    _____

    _____

    _____

    _____

4. What did I do differently today that benefitted the relationship with myself and contributed to BFF?

_____
_____
_____
_____
_____

5. What were my returning unhelpful thoughts and how did I deal with them?

_____
_____
_____
_____

6. What was my happiness level today? (0 – 10) and what was the main contributor?

_____
_____
_____
_____
_____

Daily Mindset Practice Sheet

Day nr: 18   Date: _____

1. What are three things I am grateful for today?

    a. _____

    b. _____

    c. _____

2. What are three things I am pleased with / proud of?

    a. _____

    b. _____

    c. _____

3. What did I learn today or what got confirmed?

    _____

    _____

    _____

    _____

    _____

    _____

4. What did I do differently today that benefitted the relationship with myself and contributed to BFF?

_____
_____
_____
_____
_____

5. What were my returning unhelpful thoughts and how did I deal with them?

_____
_____
_____
_____

6. What was my happiness level today? (0 – 10) and what was the main contributor?

_____
_____
_____
_____
_____

Daily Mindset Practice Sheet

Day nr: 19   Date: _____

1. What are three things I am grateful for today?

    a. _____

    b. _____

    c. _____

2. What are three things I am pleased with / proud of?

    a. _____

    b. _____

    c. _____

3. What did I learn today or what got confirmed?

    _____

    _____

    _____

    _____

    _____

    _____

    _____

4. What did I do differently today that benefitted the relationship with myself and contributed to BFF?

_____
_____
_____
_____
_____

5. What were my returning unhelpful thoughts and how did I deal with them?

_____
_____
_____
_____

6. What was my happiness level today? (0 – 10) and what was the main contributor?

_____
_____
_____
_____
_____

Daily Mindset Practice Sheet

Day nr: 20 Date: _____

1. What are three things I am grateful for today?

    a. _____

    b. _____

    c. _____

2. What are three things I am pleased with / proud of?

    a. _____

    b. _____

    c. _____

3. What did I learn today or what got confirmed?

    _____

    _____

    _____

    _____

    _____

    _____

    _____

4. What did I do differently today that benefitted the relationship with myself and contributed to BFF?

_____
_____
_____
_____
_____

5. What were my returning unhelpful thoughts and how did I deal with them?

_____
_____
_____
_____

6. What was my happiness level today? (0 – 10) and what was the main contributor?

_____
_____
_____
_____
_____

Daily Mindset Practice Sheet

Day nr: 21   Date: _____

1. What are three things I am grateful for today?

    a. _____

    b. _____

    c. _____

2. What are three things I am pleased with / proud of?

    a. _____

    b. _____

    c. _____

3. What did I learn today or what got confirmed?

    _____

    _____

    _____

    _____

    _____

    _____

Daily Practice

4. What did I do differently today that benefitted the relationship with myself and contributed to BFF?

_____
_____
_____
_____
_____

5. What were my returning unhelpful thoughts and how did I deal with them?

_____
_____
_____
_____

6. What was my happiness level today? (0 – 10) and what was the main contributor?

_____
_____
_____
_____
_____

Weekly Mindset Summary Sheet

Week nr: 3   Date: _____

1. What are three things I am grateful for this week?

    a. _____

    b. _____

    c. _____

2. What are three things I am pleased with / proud of??

    a. _____

    b. _____

    c. _____

3. What is my most important learning this week or what got confirmed?

    _____
    _____
    _____
    _____
    _____
    _____

4. What did I do differently today that benefitted the relationship with myself and contributed to BFF?

_____

_____

_____

_____

_____

5. What were my returning unhelpful thoughts this week and what was the most effective way I dealt with them?

_____

_____

_____

_____

6. What was my happiness level this week? (0 – 10) and what was the main contributor?

_____

_____

_____

_____

_____

Daily Mindset Practice Sheet

Day nr: 22   Date: _____

1. What are three things I am grateful for today?

    a. _____

    b. _____

    c. _____

2. What are three things I am pleased with / proud of?

    a. _____

    b. _____

    c. _____

3. What did I learn today or what got confirmed?

    _____

    _____

    _____

    _____

    _____

    _____

    _____

4. What did I do differently today that benefitted the relationship with myself and contributed to BFF?

_____
_____
_____
_____
_____

5. What were my returning unhelpful thoughts and how did I deal with them?

_____
_____
_____
_____

6. What was my happiness level today? (0 – 10) and what was the main contributor?

_____
_____
_____
_____
_____

Daily Mindset Practice Sheet

Day nr: 23   Date: _____

1. What are three things I am grateful for today?

    a. _____

    b. _____

    c. _____

2. What are three things I am pleased with / proud of?

    a. _____

    b. _____

    c. _____

3. What did I learn today or what got confirmed?

    _____

    _____

    _____

    _____

    _____

    _____

    _____

4. What did I do differently today that benefitted the relationship with myself and contributed to BFF?

_____
_____
_____
_____
_____

5. What were my returning unhelpful thoughts and how did I deal with them?

_____
_____
_____
_____

6. What was my happiness level today? (0 – 10) and what was the main contributor?

_____
_____
_____
_____
_____

Daily Mindset Practice Sheet

Day nr: 24   Date: _____

1. What are three things I am grateful for today?

    a. _____

    b. _____

    c. _____

2. What are three things I am pleased with / proud of?

    a. _____

    b. _____

    c. _____

3. What did I learn today or what got confirmed?

   _____
   _____
   _____
   _____
   _____
   _____

4. What did I do differently today that benefitted the relationship with myself and contributed to BFF?

_____
_____
_____
_____
_____

5. What were my returning unhelpful thoughts and how did I deal with them?

_____
_____
_____
_____

6. What was my happiness level today? (0 – 10) and what was the main contributor?

_____
_____
_____
_____
_____

Daily Mindset Practice Sheet

Day nr: 25   Date: _____

1. What are three things I am grateful for today?

    a. _____

    b. _____

    c. _____

2. What are three things I am pleased with / proud of?

    a. _____

    b. _____

    c. _____

3. What did I learn today or what got confirmed?

    _____

    _____

    _____

    _____

    _____

    _____

    _____

4. What did I do differently today that benefitted the relationship with myself and contributed to BFF?

_____
_____
_____
_____
_____

5. What were my returning unhelpful thoughts and how did I deal with them?

_____
_____
_____
_____

6. What was my happiness level today? (0 – 10) and what was the main contributor?

_____
_____
_____
_____
_____

Daily Mindset Practice Sheet

Day nr: 26   Date: _____

1. What are three things I am grateful for today?

    a. _____

    b. _____

    c. _____

2. What are three things I am pleased with / proud of?

    a. _____

    b. _____

    c. _____

3. What did I learn today or what got confirmed?

    _____

    _____

    _____

    _____

    _____

    _____

    _____

4. What did I do differently today that benefitted the relationship with myself and contributed to BFF?

_____
_____
_____
_____
_____

5. What were my returning unhelpful thoughts and how did I deal with them?

_____
_____
_____
_____

6. What was my happiness level today? (0 – 10) and what was the main contributor?

_____
_____
_____
_____
_____

Daily Mindset Practice Sheet

Day nr: 27   Date: _____

1. What are three things I am grateful for today?

    a. _____

    b. _____

    c. _____

2. What are three things I am pleased with / proud of?

    a. _____

    b. _____

    c. _____

3. What did I learn today or what got confirmed?

    _____

    _____

    _____

    _____

    _____

    _____

4. What did I do differently today that benefitted the relationship with myself and contributed to BFF?

_____
_____
_____
_____
_____

5. What were my returning unhelpful thoughts and how did I deal with them?

_____
_____
_____
_____

6. What was my happiness level today? (0 – 10) and what was the main contributor?

_____
_____
_____
_____
_____

Daily Mindset Practice Sheet

Day nr: 28   Date: _____

1. What are three things I am grateful for today?

    a. _____

    b. _____

    c. _____

2. What are three things I am pleased with / proud of?

    a. _____

    b. _____

    c. _____

3. What did I learn today or what got confirmed?

    _____

    _____

    _____

    _____

    _____

    _____

    _____

4. What did I do differently today that benefitted the relationship with myself and contributed to BFF?

_____
_____
_____
_____
_____

5. What were my returning unhelpful thoughts and how did I deal with them?

_____
_____
_____
_____

6. What was my happiness level today? (0 – 10) and what was the main contributor?

_____
_____
_____
_____
_____

Weekly Mindset Summary Sheet

Week nr: 4   Date: _____

1. What are three things I am grateful for this week?

    a. _____

    b. _____

    c. _____

2. What are three things I am pleased with / proud of??

    a. _____

    b. _____

    c. _____

3. What is my most important learning this week or what got confirmed?

    _____

    _____

    _____

    _____

    _____

    _____

4. What did I do differently today that benefitted the relationship with myself and contributed to BFF?

_____
_____
_____
_____
_____

5. What were my returning unhelpful thoughts this week and what was the most effective way I dealt with them?

_____
_____
_____
_____

6. What was my happiness level this week? (0 – 10) and what was the main contributor?

_____
_____
_____
_____
_____

Daily Mindset Practice Sheet

Day nr: 29   Date: _____

1. What are three things I am grateful for today?

    a. _____

    b. _____

    c. _____

2. What are three things I am pleased with / proud of?

    a. _____

    b. _____

    c. _____

3. What did I learn today or what got confirmed?

    _____

    _____

    _____

    _____

    _____

    _____

    _____

4. What did I do differently today that benefitted the relationship with myself and contributed to BFF?

   _____
   _____
   _____
   _____
   _____

5. What were my returning unhelpful thoughts and how did I deal with them?

   _____
   _____
   _____
   _____

6. What was my happiness level today? (0 – 10) and what was the main contributor?

   _____
   _____
   _____
   _____
   _____

Daily Mindset Practice Sheet

Day nr: 30   Date: _____

1. What are three things I am grateful for today?

   a. _____

   b. _____

   c. _____

2. What are three things I am pleased with / proud of?

   a. _____

   b. _____

   c. _____

3. What did I learn today or what got confirmed?

   _____

   _____

   _____

   _____

   _____

   _____

   _____

4. What did I do differently today that benefitted the relationship with myself and contributed to BFF?

___

5. What were my returning unhelpful thoughts and how did I deal with them?

___

6. What was my happiness level today? (0 – 10) and what was the main contributor?

___

Daily Mindset Practice Sheet

Day nr: 31   Date: _____

1. What are three things I am grateful for today?

    a. _____

    b. _____

    c. _____

2. What are three things I am pleased with / proud of?

    a. _____

    b. _____

    c. _____

3. What did I learn today or what got confirmed?

    _____
    _____
    _____
    _____
    _____
    _____

4. What did I do differently today that benefitted the relationship with myself and contributed to BFF?

_____

_____

_____

_____

_____

5. What were my returning unhelpful thoughts and how did I deal with them?

_____

_____

_____

_____

6. What was my happiness level today? (0 – 10) and what was the main contributor?

_____

_____

_____

_____

_____

Daily Mindset Practice Sheet

Day nr: 32   Date: _____

1. What are three things I am grateful for today?

    a. _____

    b. _____

    c. _____

2. What are three things I am pleased with / proud of?

    a. _____

    b. _____

    c. _____

3. What did I learn today or what got confirmed?

    _____

    _____

    _____

    _____

    _____

    _____

    _____

4. What did I do differently today that benefitted the relationship with myself and contributed to BFF?

_____
_____
_____
_____
_____

5. What were my returning unhelpful thoughts and how did I deal with them?

_____
_____
_____
_____

6. What was my happiness level today? (0 – 10) and what was the main contributor?

_____
_____
_____
_____
_____

Daily Mindset Practice Sheet

Day nr: 33   Date: _____

1. What are three things I am grateful for today?

    a. _____

    b. _____

    c. _____

2. What are three things I am pleased with / proud of?

    a. _____

    b. _____

    c. _____

3. What did I learn today or what got confirmed?

    _____

    _____

    _____

    _____

    _____

    _____

    _____

4. What did I do differently today that benefitted the relationship with myself and contributed to BFF?

_____
_____
_____
_____
_____

5. What were my returning unhelpful thoughts and how did I deal with them?

_____
_____
_____
_____

6. What was my happiness level today? (0 – 10) and what was the main contributor?

_____
_____
_____
_____
_____

Daily Mindset Practice Sheet

Day nr: 34   Date: _____

1. What are three things I am grateful for today?

    a. _____

    b. _____

    c. _____

2. What are three things I am pleased with / proud of?

    a. _____

    b. _____

    c. _____

3. What did I learn today or what got confirmed?

    _____

    _____

    _____

    _____

    _____

    _____

    _____

4. What did I do differently today that benefitted the relationship with myself and contributed to BFF?

___

5. What were my returning unhelpful thoughts and how did I deal with them?

___

6. What was my happiness level today? (0 – 10) and what was the main contributor?

___

Daily Mindset Practice Sheet

Day nr: 35   Date: _____

1. What are three things I am grateful for today?

    a. _____

    b. _____

    c. _____

2. What are three things I am pleased with / proud of?

    a. _____

    b. _____

    c. _____

3. What did I learn today or what got confirmed?

    _____

    _____

    _____

    _____

    _____

    _____

4. What did I do differently today that benefitted the relationship with myself and contributed to BFF?

_____
_____
_____
_____
_____

5. What were my returning unhelpful thoughts and how did I deal with them?

_____
_____
_____
_____

6. What was my happiness level today? (0 – 10) and what was the main contributor?

_____
_____
_____
_____
_____

Weekly Mindset Summary Sheet

Week nr: 5   Date: _____

1. What are three things I am grateful for this week?

    a. _____

    b. _____

    c. _____

2. What are three things I am pleased with / proud of??

    a. _____

    b. _____

    c. _____

3. What is my most important learning this week or what got confirmed?

    _____

    _____

    _____

    _____

    _____

    _____

4. What did I do differently today that benefitted the relationship with myself and contributed to BFF?

_____
_____
_____
_____
_____

5. What were my returning unhelpful thoughts this week and what was the most effective way I dealt with them?

_____
_____
_____
_____

6. What was my happiness level this week? (0 – 10) and what was the main contributor?

_____
_____
_____
_____
_____

Daily Mindset Practice Sheet

Day nr: 36   Date: _____

1. What are three things I am grateful for today?

    a. _____

    b. _____

    c. _____

2. What are three things I am pleased with / proud of?

    a. _____

    b. _____

    c. _____

3. What did I learn today or what got confirmed?

    _____

    _____

    _____

    _____

    _____

    _____

4. What did I do differently today that benefitted the relationship with myself and contributed to BFF?

_____
_____
_____
_____
_____

5. What were my returning unhelpful thoughts and how did I deal with them?

_____
_____
_____
_____

6. What was my happiness level today? (0 – 10) and what was the main contributor?

_____
_____
_____
_____
_____

Daily Mindset Practice Sheet

Day nr: 37   Date: _____

1. What are three things I am grateful for today?

    a. _____

    b. _____

    c. _____

2. What are three things I am pleased with / proud of?

    a. _____

    b. _____

    c. _____

3. What did I learn today or what got confirmed?

    _____

    _____

    _____

    _____

    _____

    _____

    _____

4. What did I do differently today that benefitted the relationship with myself and contributed to BFF?

_____
_____
_____
_____
_____

5. What were my returning unhelpful thoughts and how did I deal with them?

_____
_____
_____
_____

6. What was my happiness level today? (0 – 10) and what was the main contributor?

_____
_____
_____
_____
_____

Daily Mindset Practice Sheet

Day nr: 38   Date: _____

1. What are three things I am grateful for today?

    a. _____

    b. _____

    c. _____

2. What are three things I am pleased with / proud of?

    a. _____

    b. _____

    c. _____

3. What did I learn today or what got confirmed?

    _____

    _____

    _____

    _____

    _____

    _____

4. What did I do differently today that benefitted the relationship with myself and contributed to BFF?

_____
_____
_____
_____
_____

5. What were my returning unhelpful thoughts and how did I deal with them?

_____
_____
_____
_____

6. What was my happiness level today? (0 – 10) and what was the main contributor?

_____
_____
_____
_____
_____

Magical ME

Daily Mindset Practice Sheet

Day nr: 39   Date: _____

1. What are three things I am grateful for today?

    a. _____

    b. _____

    c. _____

2. What are three things I am pleased with / proud of?

    a. _____

    b. _____

    c. _____

3. What did I learn today or what got confirmed?

    _____

    _____

    _____

    _____

    _____

    _____

    _____

4. What did I do differently today that benefitted the relationship with myself and contributed to BFF?

_____

_____

_____

_____

_____

5. What were my returning unhelpful thoughts and how did I deal with them?

_____

_____

_____

_____

6. What was my happiness level today? (0 – 10) and what was the main contributor?

_____

_____

_____

_____

_____

Daily Mindset Practice Sheet

Day nr: 40   Date: _____

1. What are three things I am grateful for today?

    a. _____

    b. _____

    c. _____

2. What are three things I am pleased with / proud of?

    a. _____

    b. _____

    c. _____

3. What did I learn today or what got confirmed?

    _____

    _____

    _____

    _____

    _____

    _____

    _____

4. What did I do differently today that benefitted the relationship with myself and contributed to BFF?

_____
_____
_____
_____
_____

5. What were my returning unhelpful thoughts and how did I deal with them?

_____
_____
_____
_____

6. What was my happiness level today? (0 – 10) and what was the main contributor?

_____
_____
_____
_____
_____

Daily Mindset Practice Sheet

Day nr: 41   Date: _____

1. What are three things I am grateful for today?

    a. _____

    b. _____

    c. _____

2. What are three things I am pleased with / proud of?

    a. _____

    b. _____

    c. _____

3. What did I learn today or what got confirmed?

    _____

    _____

    _____

    _____

    _____

    _____

4. What did I do differently today that benefitted the relationship with myself and contributed to BFF?

_____

_____

_____

_____

_____

5. What were my returning unhelpful thoughts and how did I deal with them?

_____

_____

_____

_____

6. What was my happiness level today? (0 – 10) and what was the main contributor?

_____

_____

_____

_____

_____

Daily Mindset Practice Sheet

Day nr: 42   Date: _____

1. What are three things I am grateful for today?

    a. _____

    b. _____

    c. _____

2. What are three things I am pleased with / proud of?

    a. _____

    b. _____

    c. _____

3. What did I learn today or what got confirmed?

    _____
    _____
    _____
    _____
    _____
    _____
    _____

4. What did I do differently today that benefitted the relationship with myself and contributed to BFF?

_____
_____
_____
_____
_____

5. What were my returning unhelpful thoughts and how did I deal with them?

_____
_____
_____
_____

6. What was my happiness level today? (0 – 10) and what was the main contributor?

_____
_____
_____
_____
_____

Weekly Mindset Summary Sheet

Week nr: 6   Date: _____

1. What are three things I am grateful for this week?

    a. _____

    b. _____

    c. _____

2. What are three things I am pleased with / proud of?

    a. _____

    b. _____

    c. _____

3. What is my most important learning this week or what got confirmed?

    _____
    _____
    _____
    _____
    _____
    _____

4. What did I do differently today that benefitted the relationship with myself and contributed to BFF?

_____
_____
_____
_____
_____

5. What were my returning unhelpful thoughts this week and what was the most effective way I dealt with them?

_____
_____
_____
_____

6. What was my happiness level this week? (0 – 10) and what was the main contributor?

_____
_____
_____
_____
_____

Magical ME Mindset Summary Sheet

Date: _____

1. What are three things I am most grateful for in general?

    a. _____

    b. _____

    c. _____

2. What are three things I am pleased with / proud of about me?

    a. _____

    b. _____

    c. _____

3. What is my most important learning during this process or what got confirmed?

    _____

    _____

    _____

    _____

    _____

    _____

4. What are the most significant changes benefitting the relationship with myself as my BFF?

___

5. Which unhelpful thought patterns have changed and what was the most effective way I dealt with them?

___

6. What is the change in my general happiness and what are the main contributors?

___

Chapter 19
Taking Stock Again

Congratulations. You have done a great job, sticking with it, putting an effort in and getting to the end of 6 weeks of consistency in effort, observation, challenging yourself and …. Becoming your own BFF. That is what it is all about.

You are in a better place.

You deserve it.

Don't slip, keep going and keep being happy.

And for the record, just mark your changes again.

Answer the following questions with a number between 0 and 10. Zero means that you don't recognise this situation and 10 means it is overwhelmingly true. The numbers in between indicate the strength of its influence or impact.

There is no judgement.

It just is what it is.

Magical ME

	0 - 10
1. I am critical of myself	
2. I compare myself to others and feel less good, clever or pretty	
3. Other people are mor important than me	
4. I beat myself up	
5. I am a perfectionist	
6. I can't say no	
7. I doubt my decisions	
8. I have high expectations of myself	
9. I am concerned what other people think of me	
10. I ruminate	

Notes / journal

Epilogue

Often the devil is in the detail, small changes get you where you want to be without too much effort and life can look harder than it really is or needs to be.

Baby steps.

I love them.

I hope you love the ones that were presented in this book too.

Take it easy, keep working on your awareness, stop judging, especially yourself, do the practices, journal about your experiences and you will change the relationship with yourself beyond belief.

You deserve to be your own BFF.

You deserve a happy and fulfilling life.

There is more to come, so look out for the next ones in the series 'Make your life magical with easy baby steps', the following titles are available or on their way:

All of them are tuned into supporting you to create a happier life.

- Magical ME – Build A Healthy Relationship With Yourself
- Magical WORDS – Become A Better Communicator
- Magical US – Create Healthy Relationships
- Magical CONFIDENCE – Be Grounded And Have Self-Esteem
- Magical SPACE- Cut Clutter In Mind And Life
- Magical CALM – Defy Stress And Anxiety

Get in touch if you have questions or remarks, post a review on Amazon, gift a copy to a friend who might need it.

With love,
Mariette

Dr Mariette Jansen

Email: mariette@drdestress.co.uk

Website

www.drdestress.co.uk

Free Coaching Session via

https://mariettejansencoaching.youcanbook.me/

Stay in touch via my weekly email 'Seriously uplifting tips from the coaching couch'

http://eepurl.com/dsYStT

Printed in Great Britain
by Amazon